Easter

Easter

Winston Press

Library of Congress Catalog Card Number: 83-60879

Printed in Italy

ISBN 0-86683-826-0
ISBN 0-86683-811-2 (PBK)

Winston Press, Inc.
430 Oak Grove
Minneapolis MN 55403

Lodovico Mazzolino (c.1480-c.1528)
The Incredulity of St Thomas (detail)
Gallerie Borghese, Rome

Half title: Albrecht Altdorfer (1480-1538)
The Resurrection of Christ (detail)
Kunsthistorisches Museum, Vienna

Frontispiece: Marco Pina da Siena (1525-88)
The Ascension
Gallerie Borghese, Rome

Extracts from the Authorized King James
Version of the Bible, which is Crown
Copyright in England, are reproduced by
permission of Eyre & Spottiswoode, Her
Majesty's Printers.

Contents

The Last Supper

Giotto di Bondone (c.1267-1337)
The Last Supper
Alte Pinakothek, Munich

AND he said, Go into the city to such a man, and say unto him, The Master saith, My time is at hand; I will keep the passover at thy house with my disciples.

MATTHEW 26·18

AND in the evening he cometh with the twelve.

And as they sat and did eat, Jesus said, Verily I say unto you, One of you which eateth with me shall betray me.

MARK 14·17-18

AND as they were eating, Jesus took bread, and blessed it, and brake it, and gave it to the disciples, and said, Take, eat; this is my body.

And he took the cup, and gave thanks, and gave it to them, saying, Drink ye all of it;

For this is my blood of the new testament, which is shed for many for the remission of sins.

MATTHEW 26·26-28

Juan de Juanes (1523-79)
The Last Supper
Prado, Madrid

Giovanni Battista Tiepolo (1696-1770)
The Last Supper (detail)
Louvre, Paris

Jacopo Bassano (1516-92)
The Last Supper
Gallerie Borghese, Rome (Scala)

BUT I say unto you, I will not drink henceforth of this fruit of the vine, until that day when I drink it new with you in my Father's kingdom.

And when they had sung an hymn, they went out into the mount of Olives.

MATTHEW 26·29-30

The Garden of Gethsemane

Andrea Mantegna (1431-1506)
The Agony in the Garden (detail)
National Gallery, London

AND he went forward a little, and fell on the ground, and prayed that, if it were possible, the hour might pass from him.

And he said, Abba, Father, all things are possible unto thee; take away this cup from me: nevertheless not what I will, but what thou wilt.

And he cometh, and findeth them sleeping, and saith unto Peter, Simon, sleepest thou? couldest not thou watch one hour?

MARK 14·35-37

WATCH ye and pray, lest ye enter into temptation. The spirit truly is ready, but the flesh is weak.

And again he went away, and prayed, and spake the same words.

And when he returned, he found them asleep again (for their eyes were heavy,) neither wist they what to answer him.

MARK 14·38-40

El Greco (1541-1614)
Jesus in the Garden of Gethsemane (detail)
National Gallery, London

Giovanni Bellini (c.1430-1516)
The Agony in the Garden
National Gallery, London

AND he cometh the third time, and saith unto them, Sleep on now, and take your rest: it is enough, the hour is come; behold, the Son of man is betrayed into the hands of sinners.

MARK 14·41

The Betrayal

Wolf Huber (c.1490-1553)
The Taking of Christ
Alte Pinakothek, Munich

RISE up, let us go; lo, he that betrayeth me is at hand.

And immediately, while he yet spake, cometh Judas, one of the twelve, and with him a great multitude with swords and staves, from the chief priests and the scribes and the elders.

MARK 14·42-43

AND he that betrayed him had given them a token, saying, Whomsoever I shall kiss, that same is he; take him, and lead him away safely.

And as soon as he was come, he goeth straightway to him, and saith, Master, master; and kissed him.

MARK 14·44-45

Sir Anthony van Dyck (1599-1641)
The Taking of Christ
Prado, Madrid

The Scourging of Christ

AND the soldiers plaited a crown of thorns, and put it on his head, and they put on him a purple robe.

JOHN 19·2

El Greco (1541-1614)
Christ Stripped of His Garments (detail)
Alte Pinakothek, Munich

Titian (c.1487-1576)
The Scourging of Christ
Alte Pinakothek, Munich

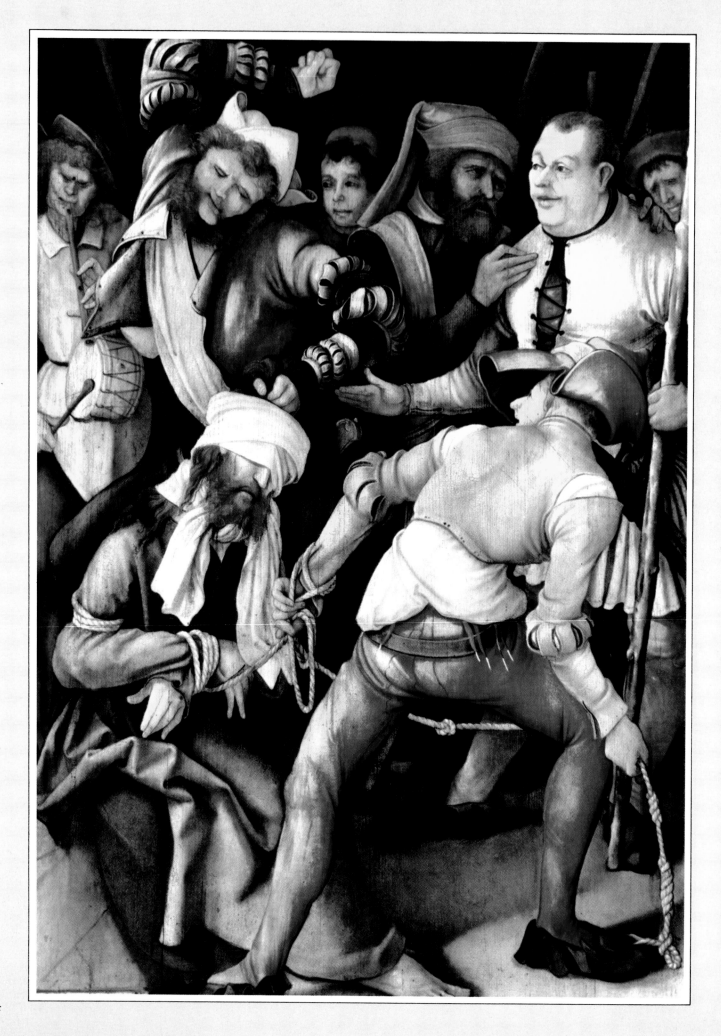

AND they spit upon him, and took the reed, and smote him on the head.

MATTHEW 27·30

BUT they cried out, Away with him, away with him, crucify him.

JOHN 19·15

Mathis Gothardt-Neithardt, known as Grünewald (c. 1460-1528)
The Derision of Christ
Alte Pinakothek, Munich

The Road to Calvary

T HEN delivered he him therefore unto them to be crucified. And they took Jesus, and led him away.

And he bearing his cross went forth into a place called the place of a skull, which is called in the Hebrew Golgotha.

JOHN 19·16-17

Simone Martini (c.1284-1344)
The Road to Calvary
Louvre, Paris

AND as they came out, they found a man of Cyrene, Simon by name: him they compelled to bear his cross.

MATTHEW 27·32

Titian (c.1487-1576)
Christ and the Cyrenian
Prado, Madrid

Raphael (1483-1520)
Christ Stumbling on the Road to Calvary (detail)
Prado, Madrid

AND there followed him a great company of people, and of women, which also bewailed and lamented him.

But Jesus turning unto them said, Daughters of Jerusalem, weep not for me, but weep for yourselves, and for your children.

LUKE 23·27-28

Raphael (1483-1520)
Christ Stumbling on the Road to Calvary
Prado, Madrid

The Crucifixion

Diego Velazquez (1599-1660)
The Crucifixion
Prado, Madrid

AND they crucified him, and parted his garments, casting lots: that it might be fulfilled which was spoken by the prophet, They parted my garments among them, and upon my vesture did they cast lots.

MATTHEW 27·35

Andrea Mantegna (1431-1506)
Calvary
Louvre, Paris

AND with him they crucify two thieves; the one on his right hand, and the other on his left.

And the scripture was fulfilled, which saith, And he was numbered with the transgressors.

MARK 15·27-28

Bernardo Daddi (active 1290-c.1349)
Calvary
Louvre, Paris

WHEN Jesus therefore saw his mother, and the disciple standing by, whom he loved, he saith unto his mother, Woman, behold thy son!

Then saith he to the disciple, Behold thy Mother!

JOHN 19·26-27

Rogier van der Weyden (c.1400-64)
Crucifixion Triptych (detail from central panel)
Kunsthistorisches Museum, Vienna

AND it was about the sixth hour, and there was a darkness over all the earth until the ninth hour.

And the sun was darkened, and the veil of the temple was rent in the midst.

LUKE 23·44-45

Lucas Cranach (1472-1553)
The Crucifixion
Alte Pinakothek, Munich

The Deposition and Burial

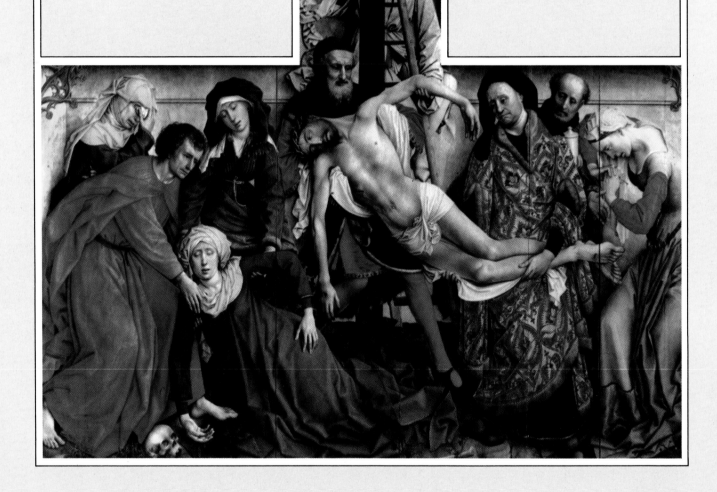

Rogier van der Weyden (c.1400-64)
The Descent from the Cross
Prado, Madrid

W HEN the even was come, there came a rich man of Arimathæa, named Joseph, who also himself was Jesus' disciple:

He went to Pilate, and begged the body of Jesus. Then Pilate commanded the body to be delivered.

MATTHEW 27·57-58

AND Pilate gave him leave. He came therefore, and took the body of Jesus.

JOHN 19·38

Rembrandt Harmensz van Rijn (1606-69)
The Descent from the Cross
Alte Pinakothek, Munich

Hugo van der Goes (active c.1467-82)
Diptych of Original Sin and Redemption (detail of mourner)
Kunsthistorisches Museum, Vienna

THEN took they the body of Jesus, and wound it in linen clothes with the spices, as the manner of the Jews is to bury.

JOHN 19·40

Albrecht Dürer (1471-1528)
Lamentation over the Dead Christ
Alte Pinakothek, Munich

AND he…laid him in a sepulchre which was hewn out of a rock.

MARK 15·46

Rogier van der Weyden (c.1400-64)
The Entombment
Uffizi, Florence

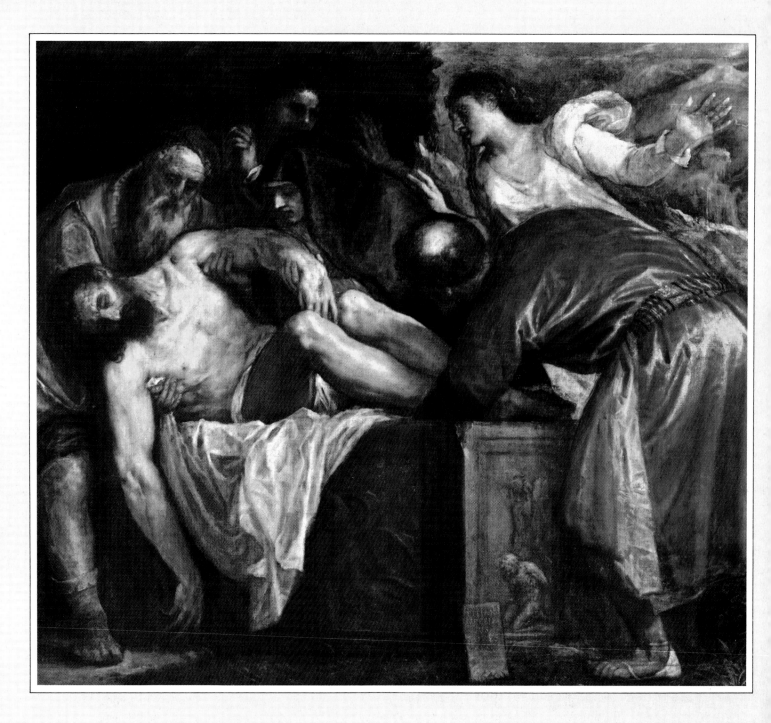

Titian (c.1487-1576)
The Tomb of Christ
Prado, Madrid

SO they went, and made the sepulchre sure, sealing the stone, and setting a watch.

MATTHEW 27·66

The Resurrection

AND behold, there was a great earthquake: for the angel of the Lord descended from heaven, and came and rolled back the stone from the door, and sat upon it.

MATTHEW 28·2

Hans Pleydenwurff (c.1420-72)
The Resurrection
Alte Pinakothek, Munich

Eugène Burnand (1850-1921)
Peter and John Running to the Tomb
Louvre, Paris (Musées Nationaux, Paris)

THEN arose Peter, and ran unto the sepulchre; and stooping down, he beheld the linen clothes laid by themselves, and departed, wondering in himself at that which was come to pass.

LUKE 24·12

Duccio di Buoninsegna (c.1255-1319)
Jesus Appearing to the Disciples
Opera del Duomo, Siena (Scala)

THEN were the disciples glad, when they saw the Lord.

Then said Jesus to them again, Peace be unto you: as my Father hath sent me, even so send I you.

And when he had said this, he breathed on them, and saith unto them, Receive ye the Holy Ghost.

JOHN 20·20-22

Christ's Appearance to Thomas

Giovanni Battista Cima da Conegliano, called Cima (c.1495-c.1517)
The Incredulity of St Thomas (detail)
Gallerie dell'Accademia, Venice

AND when they saw him, they worshipped him: but some doubted.
MATTHEW 28·17

Giovanni Battista Cima da Conegliano, called Cima (c.1495-c.1517)
The Incredulity of St Thomas
Gallerie dell'Accademia, Venice

T HEN saith he to Thomas, Reach hither thy finger, and behold my hands; and reach hither thy hand, and thrust it into my side: and be not faithless, but believing.

And Thomas answered and said unto him, My Lord and my God.

JOHN 20·27-28

Gerrit van Honthorst (1590-1656)
The Incredulity of St Thomas
Prado, Madrid

The Ascension

AND he led them out as far as to Bethany, and he lifted up his hands, and blessed them.

And it came to pass, while he blessed them, he was parted from them, and carried up into heaven.

LUKE 24·50-51

Andrea Mantegna (1431-1506)
The Ascension
Uffizi, Florence (Scala)

The Master of the St Lucy Legend (active 1480-89)
Mary Queen of Heaven (detail)
National Gallery, Washington (Samuel H. Kress Collection)

SO then after the Lord had spoken unto them, he was received up into heaven, and sat on the right hand of God.

MARK 16·19